THE COTARD DIMENSION

First published in 2011 by
The Dedalus Press
13 Moyclare Road
Baldoyle
Dublin 13
Ireland

www.dedaluspress.com

Editor: Pat Boran

Copyright © Macdara Woods, 2011

ISBN 978 1 906614 43 0

All rights reserved.
No part of this publication may be reproduced in any form or by
any means without the prior permission of the publisher.

Dedalus Press titles are distributed in the UK by
Central Books, 99 Wallis Road, London E9 5LN
and in North America by Syracuse University Press, Inc.,
621 Skytop Road, Suite 110, Syracuse, New York 13244.

Cover image © Pat Boran

The Dedalus Press receives financial assistance from
The Arts Council / An Chomhairle Ealaíon

THE COTARD DIMENSION

Macdara Woods

DEDALUS PRESS
DUBLIN, IRELAND

ACKNOWLEDGEMENTS

Grateful acknowledgement is made to the editors of the following in which a number of these poems previously appeared:

Broadsheet for Leland Bardwell (Sligo Co. Council), "çagdas irlanda siiri" (Istanbul), Census 2, Cyphers, A Garland of Words: For Maureen O'Rourke Murphy (São Paulo, Brazil), Honouring The Word: Festschrift for Maurice Harmon, The Irish Times, Light Years: Broadsheet for Pearse Hutchinson, Poetry Ireland Review, Southword, The Stony Thursday Book (Cuisle), La traductière (Paris), *This time, this place (Mayo Co. Council)* and *Voices at the World's Edge: Irish Poets on Skellig Michael,* ed. Paddy Bushe (Dedalus Press, 2010).

A postcard of the vintage ad
For Viandox
And mention of
Denfert-Rochereau
Bring back
From fifty years ago
The metro smells
Of hot dry air
The quick-quick clack
Of the door-latch
The lurching
Oblong carriages
The spicy taste
Of vermouth wine
And black tobacco
On the teeth
Tomato seeds
In the wash-hand basin
Floating up the
Plughole from
The man next door...

Do not be thinking
Of what you
Might or could
Or should have done
Or who or when
That would divide

Us from ourselves
The instant:
There is adolescence
And then there is
Adolescence

Our (adolescent)
Ageing selves
Are (part of) us
With all
(And more) than
Has been said:
Why should not
We all (Old men
And women too)
Be marvellous
And ouer meruelous
Merez
Be so mad arayed

Contents

I

Ranelagh Road Revisited / 11
For Pearse Hutchinson / 13
Circles / 14
Lake / 16
Eye / 17
Snake / 18
Caltagirone / 19
Aston Quay: January 2008 / 20
Work in Progress / 22
Leland: PS From Yalta / 24
Dearcadh / 25
And There It Is: *Bom Там...* / 27
Follies / 28
Dead Light: December / 30
Song / 34

II

CLARE ISLAND / 37

III
THE COTARD DIMENSION

From The Notebooks of Dr Jules Cotard (1840–1889) / 51
That We May Go On / 54
Malaga / 56
Taken From Candide / 58

IV

LEFT-HANDED NOTES / 61

V

Mending: May 2009 / 73
Snake Reprise / 74
The Village Festive / 76
Easter Saturday 2010 / 78
The Welder Embracing Silence / 79
Blessed Thomas of Prague / 80
Maenads / 82
Ice Burning: St Sebald / 83
Istanbul Arrival / 85
Overview / 86
In The Light of Whipple's Moon / 87
In May The Park And Me Revisited / 89

NOTES / 90

I

I take the universal and make it personal. The only true poetical and magical exchanges that occur in this life occur between two people. Sometimes it doesn't get that far. Often, the true glory of existence is confined to individual consciousness. That's okay. Let us live for the beauty of our own reality.
—Tom Robbins, *Even Cowgirls Get the Blues*

Ranelagh Road Revisited

1.
Again I heard the horse
Last week
Again it caught me by surprise
Hoofbeats
On the hard street

A space between the notes
And then
The fading into silence
The silences between the things
That come to mind …

A single summer voice
One night in 1990
Going home alone
Olé Olé Olé Olé
Reaching
Over the roof-tops
In through my window

2.
This present Monday
There was almost nothing:
Nothing from the roof
No rattling in the attic
Only the hazy separated blurs
Almost a whisper
All night
Of rain on the glass

On Tuesday night
The wind swept in
And filled the space with hugeness

3.

Three times last night
In the small hours
The horse went trotting up the road
Hoofbeats on glass
In the rain

I heard
The summer voices
Underneath my window
Young couples and late-night drinkers
Sitting on the steps
Discoursing
Devouring the eclipse:

The rusty moon
The colour of dried blood

4.

We think
The things we know
Will last forever:

The young woman
In the house next door
To this
Has died today aged thirty-one

For Pearse Hutchinson

The beast of Yucca Flats
Poor beast
Staggering round in circles
Mad as a crab in the sun

And the nightmare *rose lutin*
Poor elf
Working in the dark
On the chests of sleeping dreamers

The last gaunt plastic bags
Snared in the trees
In the rain
Till the coming of Spring

And in the night-time Cities of Light
Obsidian glass—
The dancers
Waiting silent in the streets

Circles

do JM agus PD Portlaoise

The stillness
reminds me of something

*seven wild birds
in a circle*

Scythian kurgans

Dead horsemen
on dead horses
guarding a dead man buried

hunched rider in the middle

Tonnage
of Stonehenge

Stone heads
on Easter Island
telling us where they want to go

*like the birds
constrained*

Newgrange

My grandmother
15 miles away
with the sun at Easter dancing on the ceiling

burial places

Circles
and machines—
circles within circles

turning the handle
to move around the sun

Lake

A natural low terrain
gouged by ice
water flowing

Downstream
deep and clean
free of sediment

Fills in and forms
a wetland
eventually meadow

Eye

Show not tell
its central
pitiless detachment

Black hole
outpouring
constant focus

Shrinks
chews up the universe
consuming it

Snake

This is
where we found the skin a snake had sloughed

and that the destination of all journeys
is astonishment
and touch

to get there in the end

red blood and spit

black feathers in the sun

It is the snake itself that's green
and not the skin

Tavernelle di Panicale

Caltagirone

Christmas cribs in all the churches
Flowers on the giant staircase
Wooden spinning-tops for sale
And the winter-light ceramic glaze

Who are these familiar strangers
Who come home to us?
Whispers and children both
Come from so far distant

The wind is blowing the cyclamens
By the Bridge of San Francesco
And the statue of Gualtierra now
Repeating Sicilian Vespers

Aston Quay: January 2008

Look closely at this streetscape
now
to underline it
see it as it is
As it is? for now and not
for *As it is*
as when you see it in your head
Commercial icons

Burn Our Ear Off
where once
the multi-coloured rays
fanned out from *Bovril*
into the sky
above the Ballast Office

Drays and barges
and the smell and taste
of big red copper pennies
for the slot machines
in the Fun Palace

And tiny on Eden Quay
the missing Astor Cinema:

Where I saw (*He saw*)
I saw
The Wages of Fear
Ballad of a Soldier
The Cranes are Flying

Fanfan La Tulipe
Les Enfants du Paradis
Casque D'Or Golden Marie
flicker of shadows
of shadows

My breath tightens
along the river
Wind and gulls
May it not be lost
May it not be lost forever

Work in Progress

I am of an age
when young women in shops
tell me to put my change
out of sight
... *Now put that away*
before you get outside

An age when lovers
send back letters
that I wrote them
forty years before:

These forty years
of wilderness
with no invitation to the feast
no printed music
but the shapes of crows
upon the air:
like Cathal Buí
I'll scratch my poems on a wall

Walls that grow
without our noticing
until it is too late
to keep the yellow bird afloat
Old images
on matching memories
Like Johnny Cash at the last:

It has taken long enough
to come to this:
to catch ourselves on—

Would you ever fuck off
I say to truth

Would you ever begone
And fuck away off out of that
with yourself?

Lá Fhéile Bhríde 2008

Leland: PS From Yalta

For Lissadell read Leland
my dearest long-term-lea-land-by-the-sea
where you've so well touched shore
home free
and I still making for Astapovo

There was a house in Leeson Street
and they called it 33 ...
Keep it up for twenty years the poetry
Kavanagh's words to me
in your front room

Keep spinning spinning never stop
you told me then
as you've been spinning since dear love
with your trampoline and music—
just keep on buying those pianos

Dearcadh

after Eoin Mac Lochlainn's Exhibition

Shining orrery
Black helicopter
Turning to the sun

Stag beetle
Shellacked gondola
Patent leather

If I could find

Black polish
And the smell of it
Black lead

Black Eyes
And Moscow Nights
Distended pupils

the whisper

Soot on a wall
Burnt sugar
My friend the scorpion

Charred wood
Black bile
Black blood

that runs through this

Black cloth
Black leather breviaries
Black wings

The darkness
Of the pit
Beneath the lake

the making

Darkness
Dumb
In the back of the mouth

The black black
Water
Where there is no air

And There It Is: *Вот Там...*

As I remembered it
Linz of the silent trams
That could so well knock down
An ageing gent
With ears unsure
And eyes grown faint

On the glide between
The Hauptplatz to
The Ursulines and Klosterhof
They pass up and down
Like busy toys
Rehearsing for Christmas

And the silence is lethal
Oiled and lethal as when
You have left yourself
Abandoned in a far-off place
And wait for a word
Or the touch of a breath

Follies

1.

Trimalchio my neighbour
The richest man in Umbria
With tooth and claw and JCB
Carved out a hillside and a stream
And made a landscaped
Avenue of trees and street lamps
His private public-garden

2.

In the latter end of my life
Remembering six years studying Greek
Absurd to be in Athens
Observing
The Parthenon through a periscope

3.

The fencing Venetian cellist
leaps on-stage in San Vidal
dancing with the cello
swishes some quick rapier
slashes with the bow
between two Irish fiddlers
all Perugino rolling eyes
St Theresa in ecstasy:
Grapes in a dancer's shoes

4.

I came from where it started—
a running primal ooze
in the ditch at the end of the haggard

And oh to be lying perfect now
in those Dublin underwater gardens
that bloom in Summer
with orchid greenery
in the bed of the Grand Canal

Dead Light: December

Tá sé fuar arsa an seanduine
Is é atá arsa Séimí
Fuar fuar
   —Seamus Ó Grianna, *Caisleán Óir*

i

I have been here before
In the long wet yellow winter
Strands of grass

And crows in the trees above:
Then too I felt like starting over
Unable to catch

The present moment:
Seeing that
There is no present moment

After all
No present language
Just the past and future

Travelling in opposite directions
Rushing further outwards
To the edge

And start of things:
That quick spasmodic clutch of urgency
Spilling

Into open ground
All blood and bone and hope
All past and future

All one and none:
And burning here an eager moment
Been and gone

The same: spat out to find
And drowning in
That ocean that we cannot enter

ii

Imperfect story of the Voyage
When time is bent
And calculation fails

Even in the daily
Present tense
That colluding social point

As near as we can come
To now:
To go to sleep at twenty one

And wake at sixty
Alone or with
Another head upon the pillow:

Not much comfort
For a stoic
I gCaisleán Óir or anywhere

Else but what there is
I'll take
Rise once more from the pit

And I who haven't been drunk
In thirty years
Can call to mind

Being on the road in Spain
at twenty-one: being
Young in Spain in Spanish boots

iii

My hands two yellow creatures
On the page
Like lizards hold the book

While those other poor bare creatures
Dip and thrust
Around the margins

Swaying and moaning
Gasping
Sucking licking faking

A hundred thousand times an hour
Like piston heads:
Spéir-bhean or *aisling*

Lena cam seang geal—
An tusa Helen nó Venus gleóite:
Ireland of the present times

A voice remembered
O flower of the amber locks?
Or the bare-breasted

Snake goddess of Crete
I found in the parlour book-case
Long ago in County Meath:

The stinging nettles
And the naked female satyr waiting
In the thistles in the field

Song

Air: Dicey Reilly, slowly

Rose from my bed to mend my head
And fumbled out the door
Into the street to find relief
As many times before
With one sleeve on and one shoe off
Astray in time direction lost
And the start of my ruin was rising early

Still searching for the Angel
I went walking through despair
And when we met she told me
That I lived in disrepair
It's clear said she you're sorely pressed
Out here again and half undressed
Oh the start of my ruin was rising early

I thought that life was love revealed
That everyone agreed
That no one there intended harm
Kind lilies of the field
Beneath my feet no stones of doubt
Until the tide of youth went out
When the start of my ruin was rising early

I learned the cost of what I'd lost
But learning comes too late
So little time for love or rhyme
With the Piper at the Gate

To wreak in full the banishment
Of all who don't put by the rent
And the start of my ruin was rising early

And thus the years have come undone
To leave me walking still
Along the docks and promenades
In the morning river chill
There's no going back I must go on
Each night and day pass through the dawn
For the start of my ruin was rising early

II

Clare Island

Quand irons-nous, par delà les grèves et les monts
—Arthur Rimbaud, *Saison En Enfer*

i

Deep in the unknown
empty quarter
of that country

There is a lake
and in the middle of the lake
there is an island

And in the middle
of the island
stands a mountain

And from its top
the oceans of the world
are visible:

We are less different
from each other
than islands from the land

ii

This is how we
came here
like the cormorant

Inhabiting two species
the water and
the stone walls on the mountain

Peruvian marks
of lazy-beds
stretched all across the countryside

Sailing out of Roonagh
a red queen and a white queen
dance across the bay

Coming midday
into harbour
with a thin moon overhead

iii

Strip away words
lesser words
and few

Seeing things
from nearer to the ground
to focus small:

Grains of salt
around the rock-pool
shell

Stone
flat sea and open sky
is vastness

Is silence
sound and vastness
of everything grown in

iv

Like fence-posts we stick up
on the horizon
figures masts and tower

Over and beyond
islands are like lakes inverted
upside down

The sea above
the giant hollow places
far beneath

My father told me
look at mountains paintings
upside down

Over there inside my head
still watching
light and shade on Minaun

v

When you walk around an island
you do not come back
to where you started out

This is the Imram
and the fact:
the day itself has changed

And light and time
the moving measure
of us all moved on

The ritual
of couples landing here
and setting out

At once
on bicycle and foot
to map the edges of this Ark

vi

The tower house is present
as the sea is
always present and the wind

That blows the county flags:
as sheep
as sea gulls up above the wind

And cloud and mountains
blue on grey on blue
all life: and signs of life

A shovel lying on the ground
a coal bag
underneath a bush

Blue clothes-pegs
paint tins
bags of sand cement and stones

vii

Children in the schoolyard
in the sun
girls and boys

With helmets hurleys:
a sliotar in his hand
the teacher

Is explaining all
the expertise
of poc and stance

Above the glittering sea
that stretches out
to Inishturk

And fuschia green and red
is everywhere
all Mayo red and green

viii

Please do not touch
the curraghs …
the archetypal care

As Liam Brady heard
a woman say
in Connemara

Half a century ago: *a mhac
ná bí
ag briseadh bád*

Everything comes here
by hand
by sea and history

One way and another:
Terra
Marique Potens O Maille

ix

In the cloisters
of the monastery of Oliveto
there is

A Signorelli fresco
of the angels visiting in mufti
one woman

Cutting bread
another pouring wine or water
from a jug for them:

The stuff of day to day
unconsciously rehearsed
as this

The scene repeated here
a young girl
pouring tea into a cup

x

Sand in the breaking waves
stones talking
in the flow back undertow

The low-tide rolling talk
of stones
along the beach

And the one-eyed dog
who waits
all afternoon in hope

Of stone or stick
thrown in for him to fetch
clocks off goes home

I see him next day
hard at work
driving sheep down to the boat

xi

I saw that red-gold hair before
in Philip's tomb
in Macedon

Burning red-gold
oak branch diadem and filigree
of twigs and leaves

That living artistry of wind
and chance
that crosses time

Comes down to us
like amber
floating on the Baltic sea:

A woven beehive
and a sea-wise cloth
such wisdom Ariadne brought

xii

Standing at the end of Europe
by Grace O'Malley's grave
in the Atlantic

The sea-light
seeping through the stone and windows
the fading painted figures

On the walls and ceiling
reaffirm
the unseen acts of reverence repeated

That we apply
the sanctity we bring to things
are what survive:

These damaged boars and stags
still living here
that sleek elastic hound

xiii

Going the road from
sea to sea
where the valley rises up

Between
Knockmore and Knocknaveen
and a woman on her bike

Comes cycling from the sun
none but us both
in that stupendous space

And loneliness:
the simple endless moment
of being there

And nowhere else
and knowing it: and then to leave
a moment so inhabited

xiv

Arrival and departure
all going to and coming from
in the unending

Business
of ferrying
the present to the present:

We land and gravitate a while
disperse
take credit for the weather

The wooden benches
for the passer by
stare out to sea:

A line of great stone heads
we shade our eyes
looking out to where we were

xv

They do not come again
the flashing lines
these glancing

Points of contact
if we don't
quickly press them to the page

The moments when
each frame becomes another
then another:

Making now for Roonagh
one young woman
hands round sweets

The rolling sea is luminous
a young man spends the journey
looking back

III

The Cotard Dimension

From The Notebooks of Dr Jules Cotard (1840–1889)

Is that a distorting glass
In the bathroom mirror?
No I don't believe so—Why?
When I looked just now
I didn't recognise myself:
I did not see someone else
No—but if I didn't know myself
Then who was it I saw?

There is no God or Devil
Said Mme Zero to her lover
I am dead these 40 years
Invisible before my time
Must live like this forever
An empty fairy-tale of ice
A solitary off-stage voice
And if that goes I will be lost
Water dripping on my arms
Not knowing where I've gone

As the first thing was the word
The end of everything
Is silence
The silence before the sound
And the silence after
And at the end of language

To go out like a candle
Amid owls and jackals
Or a paraffin lamp in darkness:
With the enormous silence
Full of inaudible music

From my father I inherited
A love of lonely places
Old graveyards
Empty parks and gardens
Canal banks railway lines
Country paths
The seashore in the morning:
The time my son and I
For five long days in Umbria
Saw not a single soul
Knew that we were dead
And taught the sheep
Upon the hill
Behind the house to sing

Confusion of airports
Anonymity of numbers
And in the forest
In the cool dark forest
The unreality of green:
In crowds to see and feel desire
To recognize it
To see it in a stranger's eyes:
Causes the blood to stop

Coagulate
Despite the physicality
The pumping of the heart

To be a locus only
That registers the passage
Of events: three figures
On a balcony in Mexico
A Famous Painter
A Famous Writer
A Famous Revolutionary
The accidental others in the picture
A young couple
Have not been identified:
Little Soselo loved flowers
Reached out to touch
And The Red Tsar learned to walk

And finally the brazen-calf
Automaton begins to speak:
Trifles prosecute—it roars—
Identity accelerates reflection
Mirror assures the image
And image worships mirror
In vein the nerves lust:
Will love shelve the fantasy?
The origin accesses memory
What good is this?
Why can memory not groan?

That We May Go On

Some of us are going to
Have problems
On the Last Day
With the resurrection of the flesh
Rising from the earth
Looking for teeth and foreskins
With elbows glued to ears
Our bones advancing
Backward like so much bric-à-brac

We'll have to disentangle
That: but what about the cells?
The universe of living cells
Exchanged
Those carbon miles of DNA
That we have wrapped around the world?

Tangential moments
Sending cells of light
Across the dark

I am thinking now of you
My 50-years-ago laid low
With eve-of-treatment nerves
Like Queen Titania
Played by Judi Dench
A whole midsummer and midwinter
Before a starlit audience:
And then tomorrow
When the chemicals will start again
The rude mechanicals
That keep you here a while

Our revels now are ended
But they're not—
Not this scenario
                    and not
Before we hit the Place Maubert

Malaga

> The infinite possibilities of desire.
> —Thomas Mann, *Death In Venice*

Here where I walked
On my twenty second birthday
Today I come upon surprise
L'Alegria and the *Hostal Cisneros*
Residencia Solo Habitaciones
And around the corner
Our third-floor window open still
The shutters in the afternoon half closed
Where sharp young light came in
And the women sewing opposite
Across the narrow street
Te acuerdas?
I've been here before and since
And this the first time sober
Discovering and rediscovering streets
Bits and pieces of myself
Suspended in the wind from Africa
While the Carnaval obligingly
Plays ducks and drakes with memory
Uruguayans beating drums
Mexicans dancing
Peruvians wearing stupendous hats
And I want only to be tangible
Intact in far-off sunlight
In this space here between
The things that happen and the things that are
The gap between this present moment
And the one about to be
This side of the shining mercury

To put one image on another
And to know that this is how it is
And this is how it was
Walking here and now and there
All that remains of first and last
The cities out to sea at night
Lit up: chasing
The infinite possibilities of desire

Taken From Candide

Before he passed away becoming
In the process Pangloss Bán
Weighed down with honours
I spoke to him
About that Borges poem—
The unknown book
He would never reopen
The anonymous street in Buenos Aires
He would never walk again:
Such plank-in-reason moments
As being outside at night and falling
Into stars and ice and distance
That sudden clutching cold of emptiness—

There is some perfect other
That I shall never meet
Some word that I shall never say
Though being here at all depends on both

But from himself an airy gesture
   of distaste
As from the Inns of Court—
With too much certainty for doubt
His fine-drawn face closed shut
With centuries of common sense
Imperious behind him—the cloistered
Politics of working-through the possible:
His conscious ear half-turned away
A living Eclogue in himself I thought

And more fool I: come closing time
Among the tipsy sans culottes
I watched as he sailed up and out
Into the darkness of the night
Majestic as a bull to stud
Unerring heavy practiced
Skirting his way past Saturn Mars and Venus

IV

Left-Handed Notes

*I hear and I remember
How I was
The ghost of Quasimodo
Chuting hundred-lire pieces
Thirty years ago
From hand to hand
Gout-crippled in Siena ...
And what's that other sound
From the wood?
A bad-tempered turtle dove
You said?*

*When I am alone
I speak to silence
And my aperçus go unrecorded—*

*And memory is where I am
One-fingered memory
Poking round among the ruins
Seeing again how
The Gaelic bards were right
Retiring to an unlit place
The battened hold of a boat
For composition
With a flat stone on the stomach*

*I've been here for weeks now
Semi-seduto
Sleeping in three hour bursts
And the little corner
Top-left of the wooden shutters
Gouged out by an owl
Pins everything in place
My beacon in the early morning*

A cobweb on the dawn
At night a portal to the universe
Is like a tooth the tongue
Keeps coming back to
A referential point of discipline
As this Tutorial
Strapped tight
To pull my shoulders back

As the body loosens
Moments of pain grow more intense
The gap between decision
And misdirected information
From the nerves
Widens into synapses
Of wires that do not touch:
The yard is full of pictures
On a level with my eyes
But I cannot wipe the dust away
To catch one clearly—
Enough that
Sunlight washes me with heat
As I walk slowly up and down
A Jesuit without a breviary
All things sacred
And profane
And slowly mending bone

An intelligence on sticks
Is what I have become
Cracked egg with legs
I have a plan for working out
The distance when I walk
I take a clothes-peg in my fist

From the clothesline
To the fence
Pin it there collect another
Twenty pegs a thousand metres
Dante pacing stanzas
In a single room in Florence

For years I have been conscious
Of the mockery of sounds
How pigeons here
Call out
In tones of purest Ranelagh
Fuck-off you fuck-off you
And then from the hill
Behind the house
Its Echo
Turning into stone
You're useless you're useless
With time the thought
Becomes less venomous
And now I simply acquiesce
Broken by a moving staircase
It means no more nor less
Than nightingales—
Those nightingales
I sometimes ... hardly hear
Before I try to fall asleep
Dulled down with pills

You should have wheels
On that said Pelle
In the Port in Boston
Looking at my Samson bag
Stuffed solid as a haggis

You should have wheels on that
You know my dear
You're not a cowboy any more
The prairies in the phrase
Meant general absolution
In the concrete noonday Sun
And being thus absolved
Of everything for ever more
Three years later
I set carefree wheels and foot
To step
Mid-flight ascending
From Dormition all alone
Upon the scala mobile
In Fiumicino and hurtled
Down like Lucifer to Hell—
Breaking ribs and
Clavicle
But saving neck and skull

And what surprised me most
Was how a serious rush of guilt
Almost sexual
Possessed me
That same apportioning of blame
They teach us from the start
It was my fault all mine
And mine alone
That gravity had flung me down
That the escalator steel
Was unforgiving cruel
That I had lost control
And come to grief
That I had somehow
Done this insult to myself

*As if I had not learned by now
Or having learned forgot
That life is all indifference
Of action and reaction
The single sperm
That gets there in the end
Is purposeful
And random:
Chance and meaningless*

*But still I have been waiting
For the fireflies those
Fantastic lovely architects
Of light—who build
When I am here
Manhattans out of space
And flying tiny sparks
Along the road at night
For me to walk through
In the dark
My geographical escapes
Among the insect life of Umbria
(Tell Jellinek from me
It works)
The noises and the starlit
Lovely dark—tonight
The nightingales are manic
In the cooler air
A parlement of foules
All open-throated trills
As forceful as the diva
Singing Turandot that August
Night in Macerata
Before the thunder:*

The weather
Driving home with us
Across the
Appenines into the dawn

Where does the pain go
When it eases—
Like that fantastic sound
Into the Marche night?
How many angels and etcetera ...
The shutter's broken louvres
Emphasise the light
Each morning as I wake
Edges jagged as my own
Five grinding broken ribs
And floating round
Inside my shoulder
Four dying pieces of mosaic
That were my collar bone

I heard but never saw
The bird that gnawed
Away the corner of the shutter
Athene's owl that landed
On the roof at night
A muffled sound
Like a Victorian burglar
The Hoxton Creeper
Quick and crude enough
And down to business
Lifting up the tiles to reach
The nestling sparrows underneath
Nor did I ever see a stim
Of any raven of ill-omen

Flying high above me
To the staircase—
Who ever knows
The signals of their own demise
Before
The ticking bomb explodes:
The ancient woman
In the the stream beside the road
Who washes
Bloodstained clothes

Three weeks later
And the pain starts letting go
Like ice unclenching
At the end of winter
Walking up and down the yard
I'm looking further outwards
Past the clothes-pegs
Forming and reforming
Quantum codes
Of maths and music
Red and white
In zig-zag on the fence
And past the donkey path
I've worn away—my
Mulish three mile daily dance
Of reconnection with myself

And looking outwards see again
The ruined house
Across the way—(the one
That bollox said he'd buy
Ex-British Army yes
And would-be S.A.S.

At least it didn't come to that)—
Its ruined permanence
Invincible
         and further still
Just there
And always there
The marvellous trees
The marvellous clouds

And the single
Hanging hawk upon the wind

                  May/June 2009

V

Medusa is herself the mirror
Tell Perseus

Mending: May 2009

Slow motion snow
Again the drifting poplar seeds
Across the valley

Suddenly so beautiful
The May-green hazels
And the quince

Mysterious
And around the corner that
Wild olive that we thought was dead

Blood flows
In this repeated spontaneity
Fresh growth new bone

Snake Reprise

I walked again to the German house
Up past the walnut tree
With the concrete posts
Like seats beneath—
Hieronymo to the hazel-wood
The usual mist
With nothing changed and nothing the same

The lucerne had overnight become
An olive grove
The house still tightly barred and shut
The barbed wire gone
That had been stretched across for a gate
There was no one there
No one there at all
But for a formal pair
Of high-heeled shoes on the door step

In the middle of the day
With no one there
Nothing lasts unchained said the porcupine
But the same
Never-quite-finished sunlight
Turning around and around like a clock
In the noonday silence
Of cicadas birds and childen's laughter

The trick is to assemble the mise-en-scène
One piece at a time
One foot before another—
The high-heeled shoes on the step

The empty pulsing snakeskin
Trembling in the air
The rusty wire drawing blood
And the urgency of what was there before
What might have been
Butterflies that come and go
Between the red-hot-poker and the rose

But you were there you were there
Insists the crow from the wood
No no I'm a stranger here
Sings the nightingale on the gate-post
All of us are
All of us are
Says the worker bee in the lavender

The Village Festive

Excuse me ... excuse me ...
Do you know the way to the Hellfire Club?
And I do
But it isn't here in Gulistan

Then spotting Esmé ageless
Brilliant in purple
An audience in herself
A festival of one

Belly dancers in September
Three in the street
A band on the balcony:
Catching the last of the light

Mysterious Mr Mephistos
By the dozen
One dances strumming a unicycle
Another swallows balloons

And the handsome Prince himself
Grabs images and stories
Driving a Lexus
In the back a book on Cosa Nostra

And what do I know
But that I'm ageing
And my bones are hurting—
Like General Kutuzov

Sixty years on the Ranelagh Road
A long long way
From catching pinkeens
In the vanished harbour at Portobello

Easter Saturday 2010

Hoxton Square on a sunny afternoon
And everything has been updated
Caffè Latte in Shoreditch Station
Far from Jeannie Robertson
In Hackney—the heartache
Of those preludes and romances

Things are better than they were
And truth to tell
I don't need them now at all—
The old addictions
All that time and duty spent
In a distant reckless country

Better to be a living dinosaur
The Satnav uttering directions
Tomorrow maybe
We'll take a trip to Brighton—but when
I leave for home I'll hear
Drums beating softly in the distance

The Welder Embracing Silence

I have lost the striking
Of the arc he said
Stepping back into the light
I have lost the contact
Between hand and eye

The contact between
Sound and tongue remains:
Between the image
And the brain:
But I have lost the contact

Between what I see
And what I know I am:
The thin-skinned
Living touch is gone
The cunning of the hand

Blessed Thomas of Prague

Poor Thomas of Prague arrived in Sydney
Tired and weary
Carrying an empty plastic bag
Wearing a suit gone at the knees

When he got as far as Immigration
He lowered his trousers
And adjusted himself
Said the Customs Inspector

A pensioner with 500 dollars
And little English
Overweight and bemused
Who wanted to see Hyde Park

Confused said the next Inspector
In the chain of command—
Except when he spoke in Czech
When he sounded just like anyone else

Tired and adrift
With hypothetical things to do
But no more than the rest of us
Could Thomas fully explain himself

Confused said the Chief Inspector
The man's a joke
He has insufficient money and
Has quantities of soil between his toes

Hosed down in the shower
Dressed once more in his baggy suit
They spun him around and flew him back
Still talking of seeing Hyde Park

Maenads

It is dark and there is a smell
Of pines as always
When the summer heat is over
After rain the sun is back

And symbols have become
The thing itself—this is the south
Where great matters
Are discussed in doorways

On the lower level of the parking lot
I was talking to myself
Reading circles in the dust
When the crash occurred:

Today I saw Ms Jackie Smith
Horned and elegant
Walking before me in Rapallo—
Yesterday in Po' Bandino

Falling down from the sky
Like those giant sunlit
Raindrops in September
With a couple of metres in between

Tumbling down from the hills
She was:
Head over heels and laughing
Wrestling with a mountain lion

Ice Burning: St Sebald

Word has it on the street
That he was devious
Louche they said and furbo
Given to hyperbole
Slick tricks and sleight of hand

Sneaking photos of the ceiling
In San Pantalon
Or the time at Regensburg
He crossed the Danube
On his outspread cloak

(Though not such a feat
When you think
Of Irish and Breton Saints
Sailing their Celtic Sea
In thick stone boats ...)

And then the shattered chalice
He made whole
The myriad shards of glass
Rejoining on the tiles
Impelled by an act of will

And the strange performance
In the wheelwright's
With no kindling twigs to hand
Cajoling the fire alight
With icicles for sticks

(I think he maybe just forgot
To bring the kindling in
The night before
And was unwilling now
To traipse outside in snow)

All of us have done
A thousand such impossible things
Extempore and unrehearsed
Without smoke and daggers
Or second thoughts

On an Umbrian road I met
An ostrich and two llamas
Quietly grazing the long acre
While new-felled poplars lay nearby
Beached like whales

Is not this too
A wonderment and curious—
That we buy tickets for the miracle
As we buy tickets
To the travelling circus

Istanbul Arrival

At Kabatas Pier
He steps ashore from Asia
Carrying lilies

Overview

I am here in my waiting room
Over the aural park
Hearing the announcement
Of how the railway lines
Will soon be disconnected

But how beautiful is the *luas*
That runs above the park
Beneath my bedroom window
Quick and busy in the dark
Imprinting sense on things

Up here where I turn on the light
To make a note of it
While down there nightly in the rain
The ghost-train of my life
Rolls on across the steppes

In The Light of Whipple's Moon

My first time travelling
With Ms Jackie Smith
She had but lately changed
Become a silver birch
From being a silver beech

On six-inch high stillettos
Containing within her
A continent of knowledge
And she a fleet of bark canoes
To sail the waters

Next I saw her in midwinter
In the mountains
Standing with open arms
And upthrust branches
Eloquent against the sky

In what she called
Her stance for taking off
And where are we aiming for
I asked what next? Still
Travelling light enough

To fly through light itself
She said—to get from here
To the nearest star
Or near enough to touch
It starts with a ten-day walk

Leaving the *case sparse*
Scattered houses on your left
Over the land of olives
Across the icy lake of moons
To reach the scattered disc

But first you have to learn
Perhaps by telescope
The names and constellations
Of vanished peoples
In the maproom of the Doge

All that Magnificence
Scrolled dolphins reading books
And Chiron with a dorsal fin
Turned arabesque
Ambiguous below the waist

Remember what she said
The Delphic priestess on the rock
The words before she struck
The downward stroke
That left you broken up

Once more you must move on
Align the omphalos
Just play it as it lays my dear
And after that—who knows?
The centre of the universe?

In May The Park And Me Revisited

The dropouts in the park
Are drinking Bud and Efes
I read the bottle caps
And pull-off tags from cans
Among thin plastic tubes
And tell-tale roaches
              May
Green is all about
And the community of carp
The grey friars of the lake
Are one with children
And their watchers
And all the levels in between
              And I
With those delusive ghosts
Of loneliness and failure
All the empty spaces of the years
Left unredeemed
And all the missing people
Myself among them
              When
Suddenly being here at all
Amid the sad detritus
Of bottle caps and memories
Beneath my feet
It somehow all seems *yet*—
Too beautiful to leave

2010

NOTES

P. 37, 'Clare Island'
The Clare Island sequence of fifteen poems arose out of a commission to supply text for a book of photographs of the Island, taken by Jim Vaughan, artist on the Mayo Artist Panel 2005-2006, and by the people of Clare Island themselves. The book, *This time, this place,* appeared in April 2007, from Mayo Co Council, under the Percent for Art Scheme. Project conceived and carried out by Jim Vaughan. The book may be seen online at *www.thistimethisplace.com.*

P. 53, 'From The Notebooks of Dr Jules Cotard (1840–1889)'
The brazen-calf automaton here is a conflation of the biblical golden calf, the roaring bronze bull instrument of torture and execution built by Perillos of Athens for Phalaris of Agrigentum, and most particularly the sentient computer, Alpha 60, central character/narrator in Jean-Luc Goddard's 1965 sci-fi film, *Alphaville: une étrange aventure de Lemmy Caution,* winner of the Golden Bear award in Berlin that year.

Alpha 60 can be defeated by Lemmy Caution in the end, but only because although it speaks of poetry, and quotes poetry, it cannot truly comprehend it, cannot answer a poetic riddle. In an attempt to reproduce this I allowed programmes on my own computer issue the utterances of the final stanza of my poem, with very little editing by me. The voice of Alpha 60 in the film was supplied by a man speaking through an artificial voice-box, his own having been damaged by cancer. I can hear him, I believe, delivering the computer-questions I have used: I hope so.

Dedalus Press
Poetry from Ireland and the world

Established in 1985, the Dedalus Press is one of Ireland's best-known literary imprints, dedicated to new Irish poetry and to poetry from around the world in English translation.

For further information on Dedalus Press titles, as well as audio samples and podcasts in our Audio Room, please visit **www.dedaluspress.com**.

"One of the most outward-looking poetry presses in Ireland and the UK"
—UNESCO.org

www.ingramcontent.com/pod-product-compliance
Lightning Source LLC
LaVergne TN
LVHW011429080426
835512LV00005B/334